Copyright © 2021 Patricia Moore RDN

1

Table of Contents

The Curry Cookbook: Introduction

The term curry is thought to derive from the Tamil word kari, meaning sauce. These days it refers to a variety of dishes from countries across Asia which, wet or dry, contain fish, meat or vegetables and a blend of spices and chilli. The collection of curry recipes in this book should provide some fantastic meal inspiration, whether you are after a quick midweek supper or a sophisticated, deeply flavoured party dish.

If you are looking to cut down on ordering takeaways and fancy trying your luck at making a curry at home, then you've come to the right place. The trick to a delicious curry is the spices, and letting it simmer for as long as it needs. You know, so that all those delicious flavours can blend together. We're particularly fond of a classic Chicken Tikka Masala, or Beef Massaman Curry, but also like a lighter Chickpea Curry. Fancy a side? Try our incredible Sag Aloo recipe.

The over 50 curry recipes in this book are packed full of exciting different spices and make for the perfect filling mid-week meal to comfort you after a long day.

Curry Recipes

Adriel's Chinese Curry Chicken

Ingredients

- 1 tablespoon yellow curry paste
- 1/2 cup chicken broth, divided
- 1 teaspoon white sugar
- 1 1/2 teaspoons curry powder
- 1/2 teaspoon salt
- 4 1/2 teaspoons light soy sauce
- 1 (5.6 ounce) can coconut milk
- 1 tablespoon canola oil
- 3 skinless, boneless chicken breast halves, sliced
- 2 teaspoons minced garlic
- 1 teaspoon minced fresh ginger
- 1 onion, sliced
- 2 potatoes - peeled, halved, and sliced

Directions

1. In a bowl, mash the yellow curry paste with about 2 tablespoons of chicken broth to help dissolve the paste; whisk in remaining chicken broth, sugar, curry powder, salt, light soy sauce, and coconut milk. Set aside.

2. Heat a wok or large skillet over high heat for about 30 seconds; pour in the oil. Let the oil heat until shimmering, about 30 more seconds. Stir the chicken, garlic, and ginger into the hot oil; cook and stir until the chicken has begun to brown and the garlic and ginger are fragrant, about 2 minutes. Stir in the onion and potatoes, toss all ingredients in the hot oil, and pour in the sauce mixture.

3. Bring the sauce to a boil, reduce heat, and cover the wok. Simmer until the chicken is cooked through and the potatoes are tender, 20 to 25 minutes.

Curry Coleslaw

Ingredients

- 1 head cabbage, cored and shredded
- 2 bunches green onions, chopped
- 1 (16 ounce) package frozen green peas
- 1 cup dry roasted peanuts
- 1 cup sour cream
- 1 cup mayonnaise
- 1/4 cup white vinegar
- 2 tablespoons curry powder
- 1/2 teaspoon ground ginger
- 1 teaspoon ground cayenne pepper

Directions

1. In a large bowl, mix the cabbage, green onions, peas, and peanuts.
2. In a separate bowl, mix the sour cream, mayonnaise, vinegar, curry powder, ginger, and cayenne pepper. Toss with the slaw to coat.
3. Cover and refrigerate until serving.

Fruited Tofu Curry Salad

Ingredients

- 1/2 cup white rice
- 2 cups extra-firm tofu, drained and cubed
- 1 cup yogurt
- 2 tablespoons lime juice
- 1 tablespoon curry powder
- 1 cup halved grapes
- 1 tablespoon dried cranberries
- 1/2 cup diced celery
- 3 tablespoons diced green onions
- 1/4 cup walnuts
- salt and pepper to taste

Directions

1. In a saucepan bring water to a boil. Add rice and stir. Reduce heat, cover and simmer for 20 minutes; set aside.
2. Bring a large pot of water to a boil. Cook cubed tofu for 3 minutes; drain, and set aside to cool.

3. In a bowl, blend yogurt with lime juice and curry powder; set aside. In a large mixing bowl, toss together halved grapes, cranberries, celery, green onions, walnuts, rice, and tofu. Drizzle with curry dressing, and toss until well coated. Season to taste with salt and pepper, as desired.

Fruity Curry Chicken Salad

Ingredients

- 4 skinless, boneless chicken breast halves - cooked and diced 1 stalk celery, diced
- 4 green onions, chopped
- 1 Golden Delicious apple - peeled, cored and diced
- 1/3 cup golden raisins
- 1/3 cup seedless green grapes, halved
- 1/2 cup chopped toasted pecans
- 1/8 teaspoon ground black pepper
- 1/2 teaspoon curry powder
- 3/4 cup light mayonnaise

Directions

1. In a large bowl combine the chicken, celery, onion, apple, raisins, grapes, pecans, pepper, curry powder and mayonnaise. Mix all together. Serve!

Northern Thai Curry with Chicken and Peanuts

Ingredients

- 3 large, dried red chile peppers
- 1/2 teaspoon cumin
- 1/2 teaspoon turmeric powder
- 1/2 teaspoon coriander seed
- 1/2 teaspoon ground mace
- 2 tablespoons peeled and chopped galangal
- 2 tablespoons thinly sliced lemon grass
- 1 teaspoon salt
- 1 shallot, chopped
- 2 cloves garlic, chopped
- 2 teaspoons fermented shrimp paste
- 1 tablespoon peeled and chopped fresh turmeric root
- 2 tablespoons fish sauce
- 3 tablespoons palm sugar
- 2/3 pound skinless, boneless chicken breast, cut into cubes

- 2 tablespoons vegetable oil
- 2 cups water
- 1/2 cup roasted peanuts
- 1 (2 inch) piece fresh ginger, peeled and julienned
- 2 tablespoons tamarind juice
- 2 tablespoons roasted peanuts

Directions

2. Place the chili peppers in a bowl; pour enough water over the chili peppers to cover. Allow the peppers to soak until softened, about 10 minutes; drain. Chop the peppers and set aside.

3. Grind the cumin, turmeric, coriander, and mace using a mortar and pestle into a fine powder. Add the galangal, lemon grass, salt, shallot, garlic, shrimp paste, fresh turmeric, and reconstituted chile peppers and grind into a paste. Stir the fish sauce and palm sugar into the paste. Transfer to a large bowl.

4. Add the chicken to the paste and toss to coat the chicken evenly; allow to marinate for at least 20 minutes, or up to 24 hours in the refrigerator.

5. Heat the oil in a large skillet over medium heat; cook the chicken until no longer pink in the center and the

juices run clear, 5 to 7 minutes. Stir the water, 1/2 cup peanuts, ginger, and tamarind juice into the chicken, bring to a simmer, and cook until thickened, 20 to 30 minutes. You can also cook this at a lower temperature for up to 2 hours. Garnish with 2 tablespoons peanuts to serve.

Mixed Seafood Curry

Ingredients

- 2 tablespoons vegetable oil
- 1 tablespoon minced fresh ginger root
- 1 tablespoon minced garlic
- 1 medium onion, halved and sliced
- 1 tablespoon curry paste, to taste
- 3 tablespoons lime juice
- 1 tablespoon brown sugar
- 1 (14 ounce) can light coconut milk
- 12 medium shrimp, peeled (tails left on) and deveined
- 12 sea scallops, halved
- 6 ounces asparagus, cut into 2- inch pieces

- 2 tablespoons chopped cilantro salt to taste

Directions

1. Heat the oil in a large pan over medium-high heat. Cook the ginger, garlic, and onion until the onion softens, about 2 to 3 minutes. Stir in the curry paste, lime juice, brown sugar, and coconut milk; simmer for 5 minutes. Stir in the shrimp, scallops, asparagus, cilantro, and salt; cook until the seafood is opaque, 4 to 5 minutes.

Chicken with Curry Dill Sauce

Ingredients

- 2 tablespoons butter or margarine
- 2 tablespoons all-purpose flour
- 1/8 teaspoon salt
- Dash pepper
- 1 cup milk

- 1/4 cup mayonnaise
- 1/2 teaspoon dill weed
- 1/4 teaspoon curry powder
- 6 bone-in chicken breast halves
- 1 tablespoon vegetable oil

Directions

1. In a saucepan over medium heat, melt butter. Add the flour, salt and pepper; stir until smooth. Gradually add milk and bring to a boil. Boil and stir for 2 minutes. Remove from the heat. Add the mayonnaise, dill and curry; stir until smooth. Set aside. In a skillet over medium heat, brown chicken in oil. Place in a greased shallow 3-qt. baking dish. Pour sauce over chicken. Bake, uncovered, at 350 degrees F for 50-60 minutes or until meat juices run clear.

Curry Carrot-Leek Soup

Ingredients

- 1 pound thinly sliced leeks, white parts only
- 1 pound carrots, coarsely chopped
- 2 teaspoons butter or stick margarine
- 1 medium potato, peeled and diced
- 1/2 teaspoon curry powder
- 4 cups reduced-sodium chicken broth
- 1/4 teaspoon salt
- 1/4 teaspoon pepper

Directions

1. In a large saucepan, saute leeks and carrots in butter until leeks are tender. Add potato and curry powder; cook and stir for 2 minutes. Add broth, salt and pepper; bring to a boil. Reduce heat; cover and simmer for 15-20 minutes or until the vegetables are very tender.
2. Cool slightly. Process in batches in a food processor or blender until pureed. Return to the pan; heat through.

Curry Cheddar Scrambled Eggs

Ingredients

- 1/4 teaspoon curry powder
- Salt and pepper, to taste
- 2 large eggs, beaten
- 2 tablespoons shredded Cheddar cheese
- 1/2 teaspoon margarine or butter

Directions

1. Sprinkle the curry powder, salt and pepper onto the beaten eggs; beat together until well blended. Stir in the Cheddar cheese.
2. Melt the margarine in a skillet over medium heat. Pour in the eggs, and cook, stirring constantly until firmed to desired temperature, 3 to 5 minutes.

Curry Mango Chicken

Ingredients

Chicken:

- 3 1/2 tablespoons curry powder
- 2 teaspoons minced ginger
- 2 cloves garlic, minced
- 1 pinch crushed red pepper flakes
- 1/4 teaspoon salt
- 1/4 teaspoon black pepper
- 1 teaspoon thyme
- 10 skinless chicken thighs

Rice:

- 2 cups converted long-grain white rice, rinsed
- 2 cups mango - peeled, seeded and chopped
- 1 onion, chopped
- 2 cloves crushed garlic
- 2 teaspoons minced fresh ginger root

- 1 tablespoon curry powder
- 1 pinch red pepper flakes
- 1 teaspoon salt
- 1/4 teaspoon thyme
- 10 whole allspice berries
- 3 tablespoons brown sugar
- 1 cup water
- 2 cups chicken broth
- 2 tablespoons lime juice
- 1/2 (14 ounce) can coconut milk

Directions

1. In a large bowl, stir together the curry, ginger, garlic, red pepper flakes, salt, pepper, and thyme. Place the chicken in the bowl, and coat evenly with seasoning. Cover, and marinate for 2 hours or more.

2. Preheat oven to 400 degrees F (200 degrees C).

3. In a large bowl, stir together rice, mango, onion, garlic, and ginger. Season with curry, red pepper flakes, salt, thyme, allspice berries, and brown sugar. Stir in water, broth, and lime juice. Pour into a casserole dish, and arrange the marinated chicken on top. Then pour coconut milk over the top. Cover with aluminum foil.

4. Bake in preheated oven for 1 hour. Remove foil, and cook 10 to 15 minutes more. Remove allspice berries before serving.

Chicken Chicken Curry

Ingredients

- 3 tablespoons olive oil
- 1 red onion, thinly sliced, divided salt to taste
- 1 bay leaf
- 1 tablespoon water
- 1 tablespoon ground turmeric
- 1/2 teaspoon chili powder
- 1/2 teaspoon paprika
- 2 tablespoons ground ginger
- 2 tablespoons minced garlic
- 1 tablespoon water
- 2 1/4 pounds skinless, boneless chicken breast, cut in bite-sized pieces
- 1 tomato, thinly sliced
- 1/4 teaspoon white sugar
- 3 cardamom pods, lightly crushed
- 3 whole cloves

- 1 (2 inch) cinnamon stick
- 1 tablespoon ghee (clarified butter)
- 1 tablespoon water
- 1 tablespoon ground coriander
- 1 bunch cilantro, chopped

Directions

1. Heat the olive oil in a skillet over high heat. Stir in 1/3 of the onion; cook and stir until the onion is golden brown and crisp, about 5 minutes. Season with salt. Remove the onion from the oil and drain on a paper towel-lined plate. Set aside.

2. Place the remaining 2/3 of onion and the bay leaf into the same skillet over high heat. Cook and stir until the onion has turned golden brown, about 5 minutes. Stir in 1 tablespoon of water, then add the turmeric, chili powder, paprika, ginger, and garlic. Reduce heat to medium-high and continue to cook and stir until the liquid has reduced, then stir in another tablespoon of water.

3. Place the chicken and tomato slices into the onion mixture. Season with salt and sugar. Stir in the cardamom pods, cloves, cinnamon stick, ghee, and 1

tablespoon of water. Cover and simmer on low until the liquid has reduced, 30 to 35 minutes. Stir in the coriander. Simmer until the liquid has evaporated. Sprinkle with cilantro and reserved fried onions before serving.

Olive and Chicken Curry Ingredients

CREPES

- 1 1/2 cups all-purpose flour
- 2 1/2 cups milk
- 3 eggs, beaten
- 2 tablespoons vegetable oil
- 1/2 teaspoon salt

FILLING

- 1/4 cup butter
- 1 1/4 cups diced celery
- 1 cup diced onion
- 2 tablespoons all-purpose flour
- 1 teaspoon salt
- 3/4 teaspoon curry powder
- 1 cup milk

- 2 cubes chicken bouillon
- 1/2 cup warm water
- 3/4 cup sliced black olives
- 2 1/2 cups cooked, diced chicken breast meat
- 1/4 cup freshly grated Parmesan cheese

Directions

1. To Make Crepes: In a medium bowl combine the flour, milk, eggs, oil and salt and beat together for 1 minute, until you have a smooth, thin batter.
2. Heat a lightly greased medium skillet over medium heat, pouring in a thin layer of crepe batter that covers bottom of pan. Brown on one side only, repeating until all of the batter is used. Set crepes aside.
3. To Make Filling: Melt butter in a large skillet over medium heat and saute celery and onion until just barely tender. Stir in flour, salt and curry, blending well. Dissolve bouillon in water, then pour milk and bouillon mixture into skillet, stirring until well mixed and thickened. Add olives and chicken and mix all together.
4. Preheat oven to 400 degrees F (200 degrees C).

5. Spoon some of the filling mixture onto the center of each crepe, leaving enough room to fold edges burrito-style. Fold up crepes and place in a lightly greased 9x13 inch baking dish. Sprinkle with cheese.
6. Bake in preheated oven for about 12 minutes, or until cheese is melted.

Special Beef Rendang Curry

Ingredients

- 1 pound beef round, diced
- 2 tablespoons cooking oil
- 3/4 cup dried shrimp, minced
- 1 clove garlic, minced
- 1 tablespoon chopped lemon grass
- 2 onions, chopped
- 1 3/4 cups coconut milk
- 1/2 cup red curry paste, or to taste
- 3 tablespoons turmeric powder
- 1 fresh red chile pepper, finely chopped (optional)
- 1 bunch fresh cilantro, chopped

Directions

1. This first step is to soften the beef. Place the beef in a medium saucepan, and add enough water to cover the meat. Cover, and simmer over low heat for at least an hour. Remove the beef from water, and set aside.

2. Heat the oil in a wok over medium-high heat. Add in the garlic and dried shrimp, and stir fry for a few seconds before stirring in the lemon grass and onions. Reduce heat to medium, and stir in coconut milk, red curry paste, turmeric, and chile pepper. Mix in the beef, and cover the wok. Simmer for 10 minutes over medium heat.

3. Stir in the cilantro just before serving. Save some cilantro for garnishing on top if you like.

Curry-Strawberry Chicken

Ingredients

- 1 1/2 cups Russian salad dressing
- 2 tablespoons curry powder
- 3 tablespoons dry onion soup mix
- 1/4 cup strawberry jam
- 4 skinless, boneless chicken breast half - cut into bite-size pieces

Directions

1. Mix salad dressing, curry powder, onion soup mix, and strawberry jam in a large bowl until smooth. Place chicken breast into a 9x13 inch baking dish and pour the dressing mixture on top. Cover and refrigerate overnight, or at least 1 hour before baking.
2. Preheat an oven to 375 degrees F (190 degrees C).
3. Uncover the baking dish. Bake the chicken breasts in the preheated oven until no longer pink in the center, 20 to 25 minutes.

Lamb Madras Curry

Ingredients

- Curry Paste
- 1 1/2 tablespoons coriander seeds
- 1 1/2 teaspoons cumin seeds
- 1/2 teaspoon salt
- 5 whole dried red chile peppers
- 6 fresh curry leaves
- 3 tablespoons garlic paste
- 2 teaspoons ginger paste
- 1 1/2 teaspoons ground turmeric
- 2 1/4 pounds lamb meat, cut into 1 1/2 inch cubes
- 1/2 cup ghee (clarified butter), melted
- 1/4 cup vegetable oil
- 4 onion, sliced
- 1/4 inch thick
- 1 (13.5 ounce) can coconut milk
- 2 cups water, divided

- 1 teaspoon fennel seeds
- 6 cardamom pods
- 1 cinnamon stick
- 1 1/2 teaspoons garam masala
- 1 teaspoon sugar
- 3 tablespoons warm water
- 1 tablespoon tamarind paste

Directions

1. Toast the coriander seeds over medium-low heat until they begin to turn brown and pop. Repeat the toasting process with the cumin seeds, then with the dried red peppers. Transfer each ingredient to a food processor or spice grinder as you finish. Add the salt and grind to a fine powder. Mix with the garlic and ginger to form a thick paste.

2. Sprinkle the turmeric over the lamb, stirring lightly to coat. Toast the fennel seeds as above and set aside. Heat a Dutch oven over medium heat with the ghee and vegetable oil; cook the onions until golden brown, about 10 minutes. Stir in your curry paste and fry for 1 minute. Stir in the meat and fry for 1 minute more. Pour in 2/3 of the can of coconut milk and 1 cup of

water; bring to a boil, then reduce the heat to low. Simmer for 10 minutes.

3. Stir in the remaining coconut milk and 1 cup of water, along with the cardamom pods, cinnamon stick, and toasted fennel seeds. Cover with the lid ajar and return to a simmer, cook for about 1 1/2 hours until the lamb is tender. Stir occasionally and thin with water if the sauce becomes too thick while cooking.

4. When the lamb is tender, stir in garam masala, sugar, and the tamarind paste dissolved in 3 tablespoons of water; cook 5 minutes longer, or until the sauce thickens. Remove the cinnamon stick and cardamom pods before serving.

Red Lentil Curry

Ingredients

- 2 cups red lentils
- 1 large onion, diced
- 1 tablespoon vegetable oil
- 2 tablespoons curry paste
- 1 tablespoon curry powder
- 1 teaspoon ground turmeric
- 1 teaspoon ground cumin
- 1 teaspoon chili powder
- 1 teaspoon salt
- 1 teaspoon white sugar
- 1 teaspoon minced garlic
- 1 teaspoon ginger root, minced
- 1 (14.25 ounce) can tomato puree

Directions

1. Wash the lentils in cold water until the water runs clear (this is very important or the lentils will get "scummy"),

put the lentils in a pot with water to cover and simmer covered until lentils tender (add more water if necessary).

2. While the lentils are cooking: In a large skillet or saucepan, caramelize the onions in vegetable oil.

3. While the onions are cooking, combine the curry paste, curry powder, turmeric, cumin, chili powder, salt, sugar, garlic, and ginger in a mixing bowl. Mix well. When the onions are cooked, add the curry mixture to the onions and cook over a high heat stirring constantly for 1 to 2 minutes.

4. Stir in the tomato puree and reduce heat, allow the curry base to simmer until the lentils are ready.

5. When the lentils are tender drain them briefly (they should have absorbed most of the water but you don't want the curry to be too sloppy). Mix the curry base into the lentils and serve immediately.

Devil Curry

Ingredients

- 3 tablespoons vegetable oil
- 2 tablespoons water, or as needed
- 6 red onions, chopped
- 25 chile peppers, sun-dried
- 7 candlenuts
- 1 shrimp paste
- 1 teaspoon ground turmeric
- 1 teaspoon ground ginger
- 1 teaspoon ground allspice
- 3 lemon grass
- 1 tablespoon mustard seed
- 2 cups water
- 2 1/4 pounds skinless, boneless chicken breast meat - cut into bite-size pieces
- 2 1/4 pounds potatoes
- salt to taste
- 1 tablespoon distilled white vinegar

Directions

1. Heat oil in a large skillet over medium high heat. In a medium bowl combine the onions, chile peppers, candlenuts, shrimp paste, turmeric, ginger, galangal, lemon grass and mustard seed. Blend together with a little water to form a fine paste. Add to skillet and saute until fragrant and almost dry.

2. Add 2 cups water and bring all to a boil. Add chicken and potatoes. Reduce heat and let simmer about 20 minutes, or until chicken is cooked (no longer pink inside) and curry is quite thick in consistency.

3. Add salt to taste. Remove from heat and add vinegar. Mix well and serve. This dish is best served with steamed white rice, as it is full of flavor.

Quornв„ў and Chickpea Curry

Ingredients

- 2 tablespoons vegetable oil
- 1 (12 ounce) package Quornв„ў Chicken-Style Recipe Tenders
- 1 medium onion, chopped
- 3 cloves garlic, crushed
- 1/2 teaspoon cumin seed
- 1/2 teaspoon black mustard seed
- 1 teaspoon ground turmeric
- 1 teaspoon ground cumin
- 1 teaspoon ground coriander
- 1 teaspoon chili powder
- 1 teaspoon salt
- 2 teaspoons tomato puree
- 1 (8 ounce) can chickpeas (garbanzo beans), drained
- 1 (14 ounce) can diced tomatoes
- 1 cup vegetable broth

- 1 teaspoon garam masala

Directions

1. Heat 1 tablespoon oil in a large skillet or wok over medium-high heat. Cook Quorn in oil until golden brown. Set aside.

2. Using the same pan, heat remaining 1 tablespoon oil over medium heat. Cook onion, garlic, cumin seed, and mustard seed in oil for 3 to 5 minutes, or until the onion is soft.

3. Season with ground turmeric, cumin, and coriander, chili powder, and salt. Mix in tomato puree, then stir in Quorn, chickpeas, diced tomatoes, and vegetable stock. Bring to a boil, reduce heat to medium-low, and simmer for 20 to 25 minutes. Remove from heat, and mix in garam masala.

North Indian Nepali Curry Dumplings

Ingredients

- 2 tablespoons olive oil
- 1 clove garlic, chopped
- 1 onion, sliced
- 1 tomato, diced
- salt and black pepper to taste
- 1 pinch cayenne pepper, or to taste
- 1 tablespoon chopped fresh cilantro
- 1 pound ground pork
- 1 bunch cilantro, chopped
- 1 onion, chopped
- 1 bunch green onions, chopped
- 1 tablespoon garam masala
- 1 teaspoon curry powder
- 2 cloves garlic, chopped
- 1 teaspoon ginger paste
- salt and black pepper to taste

- 2 (10 ounce) packages round dumpling wrappers

Directions

1. To make the dipping sauce, heat the olive oil in a skillet over medium heat. Stir in 1 clove of garlic and the chopped onion; cook and stir until the onion has softened and turned translucent, about 5 minutes. Stir in the tomato, salt, pepper, and cayenne pepper.

2. Cover and reduce heat to low and continue cooking for 15 minutes. Remove from heat and stir in 1 tablespoon cilantro. Pour sauce into a blender and carefully blend until smooth. Cover and refrigerate until ready to use.

3. Combine the ground pork, 1 bunch of cilantro, chopped onion, green onions, garam masala, curry powder, 2 cloves of garlic, ginger paste, salt, and pepper in a large bowl. Place a heaping teaspoon of the pork mixture in the center of a dumpling wrapper. Moisten the edge of the wrapper with a few drops of water. Fold the dumpling in half into a half moon shape. Repeat with the remaining dumplings.

4. Place a steamer insert into a saucepan, and fill with water to just below the bottom of the steamer. Cover, and bring the water to a boil over high heat. Add the dumplings, recover, and steam until cooked through, about 15 minutes. Serve with the dipping sauce.

Coconut Curry Tofu

Ingredients

- 2 bunches green onions
- 1 (14 ounce) can light coconut milk
- 1/4 cup soy sauce, divided
- 1/2 teaspoon brown sugar
- 1 1/2 teaspoons curry powder
- 1 teaspoon minced fresh ginger
- 2 teaspoons chile paste
- 1 pound firm tofu, cut into 3/4 inch cubes
- 4 roma (plum) tomatoes, chopped
- 1 yellow bell pepper, thinly sliced
- 4 ounces fresh mushrooms, chopped
- 1/4 cup chopped fresh basil
- 4 cups chopped bok choy salt to taste

Directions

1. Remove white parts of green onions, and finely chop. Chop greens into 2 inch pieces.

2. In a large heavy skillet over medium heat, mix coconut milk, 3 tablespoons soy sauce, brown sugar, curry powder, ginger, and chile paste. Bring to a boil.

3. Stir tofu, tomatoes, yellow pepper, mushrooms, and finely chopped green onions into the skillet. Cover, and cook 5 minutes, stirring occasionally. Mix in basil and bok choy. Season with salt and remaining soy sauce. Continue cooking 5 minutes, or until vegetables are tender but crisp. Garnish with remaining green onion.

Spinach Chick Pea Curry

Ingredients

- 1 tablespoon vegetable oil
- 1 onion, chopped
- 1 (14.75 ounce) can creamed corn
- 1 tablespoon curry paste
- salt to taste
- ground black pepper to taste

- 1/2 teaspoon garlic powder, or to taste
- 1 (15 ounce) can garbanzo beans, drained and rinsed
- 1 (12 ounce) package firm tofu, cubed
- 1 bunch fresh spinach, stems removed
- 1 teaspoon dried basil or to taste

Directions

1. In a large wok or skillet heat oil over medium heat; saute onions until translucent. Stir in creamed corn and curry paste. Cook, stirring regularly, for 5 minutes. As you stir, add salt, pepper and garlic.

2. Stir in garbanzo beans and gently fold in tofu. Add spinach and cover. When spinach is tender, remove from heat and stir in basil.

Tomato Curry Chicken

Ingredients

- 4 skinless, boneless chicken breast halves
- 2 tablespoons butter
- 1 onion, chopped
- 2/3 cup beer
- 1 (10.75 ounce) can condensed tomato soup
- 1 teaspoon curry powder
- 1/2 teaspoon dried basil
- 1/2 teaspoon ground black pepper
- 1/4 cup grated Parmesan cheese

Directions

1. Preheat oven to 350 degrees F (175 degrees C).
2. Place chicken in a 9x13 inch baking dish. Melt butter in a medium skillet over medium heat. Saute onion, then stir in beer, soup, curry powder, basil and pepper. Reduce heat to low and simmer for about 10 minutes, then pour over chicken.

3. Bake at 350 degrees F (175 degrees C) for 1 hour; sprinkle with cheese for last 10 minutes of baking.

Chicken Curry Party Salad

Ingredients

- 1 cube chicken bouillon
- 9 ounces skinless, boneless chicken breasts
- 9 ounces fresh mushrooms, sliced
- 1 (8 ounce) package elbow macaroni
- 1/2 cup sour cream
- 1/2 cup mayonnaise
- 1 clove garlic, chopped
- 1 teaspoon curry powder
- 1 (4 ounce) can black olives, drained and chopped
- 1 apple - peeled, cored and sliced
- 1 yellow bell pepper, thinly sliced
- 2 stalks celery, chopped
- salt and pepper to taste

Directions

1. Bring a large pot of lightly salted water to a boil; add bouillon cube and stir until melted. Add chicken and

poach for about 13 to 14 minutes. Remove chicken and leave broth in pot; cool chicken and cut into 1/2 inch chunks; reserve.

2. Add mushrooms to broth and cook over medium heat; cook for a few minutes and remove mushrooms from stock; reserve.

3. With remaining stock in pot, add some more water, if needed. Bring water to a boil and add pasta to cook for 8 to 10 minutes or until al dente; drain and discard stock. Cool pasta with running water; reserve.

4. In a small bowl, combine sour cream, mayonnaise, garlic, curry powder and salt and pepper to taste.

5. In a large bowl, combine cooled pasta, chicken, mushrooms, sour cream dressing, olives, apple, yellow bell pepper and celery; mix well. Refrigerate for at least 3 hours and serve.

Coconut Curry Pumpkin Soup

Ingredients

- 1/4 cup coconut oil
- 1 cup chopped onions
- 1 clove garlic, minced
- 3 cups vegetable broth
- 1 teaspoon curry powder
- 1/2 teaspoon salt
- 1/4 teaspoon ground coriander
- 1/4 teaspoon crushed red pepper flakes
- 1 (15 ounce) can 100% pure pumpkin
- 1 cup light coconut milk

Directions

1. Heat the coconut oil in a deep pot over medium-high heat. Stir in the onions and garlic; cook until the onions are translucent, about 5 minutes. Mix in the vegetable broth, curry powder, salt, coriander, and red pepper flakes. Cook and stir until the mixture comes to a gentle boil, about 10 minutes. Cover, and boil 15 to 20

minutes more, stirring occasionally. Whisk in the pumpkin and coconut milk, and cook another 5 minutes.

2. Pour the soup into a blender, filling only half way and working in batches if necessary; process until smooth. Return to a pot, and reheat briefly over medium heat before serving.

Four Seasons Chicken Curry

Ingredients

- 3 tablespoons vegetable oil
- 1 medium onion, chopped
- 3 cloves garlic, sliced
- 1 (1 inch) piece fresh ginger root, grated
- 1 (1 inch) piece stick cinnamon
- 3 bay leaves
- 1 tablespoon brown sugar
- 1 teaspoon coriander seeds
- 1 teaspoon fenugreek seeds
- 6 whole cloves

- 6 whole cardamom pods
- 1 teaspoon crushed red pepper flakes
- 10 whole black peppercorns
- 2 pounds skinless, boneless chicken breast halves - diced
- 3 tablespoons curry powder
- 1 1/2 cups water, or as needed
- 1 tablespoon lemon juice
- salt and pepper to taste
- 1/2 cup light cream

Directions

1. Heat the oil in a wok over medium heat, and cook the onion until lightly browned. Mix in garlic, ginger, cinnamon, bay leaves, brown sugar, coriander, fenugreek, cloves, cardamom, red pepper, and peppercorns. Cook and stir about 3 minutes. Place chicken in the wok, and cook until lightly browned. Mix in curry powder. Pour in water, and bring to a boil. Reduce heat to low, cover, and simmer 30 minutes. Add more water as necessary to keep chicken covered.

2. Mix in lemon juice, season with salt and pepper, and continue cooking at least 15 minutes. Stir in cream and remove cinnamon stick and bay leaves before serving.

Vietnamese Lemon Grass Chicken Curry

Ingredients

- 2 tablespoons vegetable oil
- 1 lemon grass, minced
- 1 (3 pound) whole chicken, cut into pieces
- 2/3 cup water; 1 tablespoon fish sauce
- 1 1/2 tablespoons curry powder; 1 tablespoon cornstarch
- 1 tablespoon chopped cilantro (optional)

Directions

1. Heat the vegetable oil in a skillet over medium heat. Stir in the lemon grass, cooking until fragrant, 3 to 5 minutes. Place the chicken into the skillet. Cook and stir the chicken until no longer pink in the center and the skin is browned, about 10 minutes. Stir in the water, fish sauce, and curry powder. Increase heat to

high and bring to a boil. Reduce heat and simmer for 10 to 15 minutes.

2. Mix cornstarch and 2 tablespoons of the curry sauce in a small bowl, until smooth. Stir cornstarch mixture into the skillet and simmer until sauce has thickened, about 5 minutes. Garnish with cilantro before serving.

Authentic Bangladeshi Beef Curry

Ingredients

- 3 tablespoons olive oil
- 1 onion, chopped
- 6 cloves garlic, minced
- 5 green chile peppers, finely sliced
- 1 teaspoon fresh ginger root - peeled, sliced, and ground into a paste
- 3 cardamom pods
- 2 whole cloves
- 1 1/2 cinnamon sticks
- 1 teaspoon ground cumin
- 1 teaspoon ground coriander
- 1 teaspoon ground turmeric
- 1 teaspoon garlic powder
- 1 teaspoon cayenne pepper

- 1 cup water
- 2 pounds boneless beef chuck, cut into 1-1/2-inch pieces

Directions

1. Heat the oil in a skillet over medium heat. Add the onion; cook and stir until the onion has softened and turned translucent, about 5 minutes. Reduce heat to medium-low, and continue cooking and stirring until the onion is very tender and dark brown, 15 to 20 minutes more.
2. Stir in the garlic, green chiles, ginger paste, cardamom pods, cloves, and cinnamon sticks. Cook and stir for an additional 3 to 5 minutes, until the garlic begins to brown.
3. Stir the cumin, coriander, turmeric, garlic powder, cayenne pepper, and water into the onions. Simmer until most of the water has evaporated and the mixture has thickened.

4. Stir in the beef chuck and cook on medium-low heat, stirring occasionally, until the meat is cooked through and tender, about 1 to 1 1/2 hours.

Slow Cooker Marmalade Curry Chicken

Ingredients

- 5 (6 ounce) boneless skinless chicken breasts
- salt and pepper, to taste
- 1 (12 ounce) jar orange marmalade
- 1/2 cup chicken stock
- 1 1/2 teaspoons curry powder
- 1/2 teaspoon ground cayenne pepper
- 1 pinch ground ginger

Directions

1. Season the chicken breasts with salt and pepper, and place into a slow cooker. Whisk together the marmalade, chicken stock, curry powder, cayenne

pepper, and ground ginger in a bowl. Pour over chicken breasts.

2. Cover, and cook on High for 3 to 4 hours, or on Low for 5 to 7 hours. Make sure to flip over the chicken breasts once during cooking.

Thai Green Curry Prawns

Ingredients

- 1/2 teaspoon ground cumin
- 1 1/2 teaspoons ground coriander
- 1 tablespoon minced fresh ginger root
- 4 teaspoons minced garlic
- 2 green chile peppers, chopped
- 3 stalks lemon grass, minced
- 1/3 cup chopped fresh cilantro
- 2 limes, juiced
- 1 lime, zested
- 2 tablespoons corn oil
- 1/4 cup corn oil

- 1/2 pound fresh green beans, trimmed
- 1 (7 ounce) can baby corn, drained
- 1 tablespoon soy sauce
- 1 (14 ounce) can coconut milk
- 3/4 pound peeled and deveined
- medium shrimp (30-40 per pound)

Directions

1. Place cumin, coriander, ginger, garlic, green chile peppers, lemon grass, cilantro, lime juice, lime zest, and 2 tablespoons of corn oil in a food processor. Blend to a smooth, thick paste. Set aside.

2. Heat 1/4 cup of corn oil in a large skillet over medium-high heat. Cook and stir green beans and baby corn for about 30 seconds. Stir in the paste, soy sauce, and coconut milk and bring to a boil.

3. Reduce heat to medium and simmer for 5 to 7 minutes, then add the shrimp. Cook the shrimp until they are bright pink on the outside and the meat is no longer transparent in the center, 3 to 5 minutes. If the sauce becomes too thick, stir in some water.

Slow-Cooker Pork and Apple Curry

Ingredients

- 2 pounds boneless pork loin roast, cut into 1-inch cubes
- 1 medium tart apple, peeled and chopped
- 1 small onion, chopped
- 1/2 cup orange juice; 1 tablespoon curry powder
- 1 teaspoon chicken bouillon granules
- 1 garlic clove, minced; 1/2 teaspoon salt
- 1/2 teaspoon ground ginger
- 1/4 teaspoon ground cinnamon
- 2 tablespoons cornstarch
- 2 tablespoons cold water Hot cooked rice
- 1/4 cup raisins; 1/4 cup flaked coconut, toasted

Directions

1. In a 3-qt. slow cooker, combine the first 10 ingredients. Cover and cook on low for 5-6 hours or until meat is tender. Increase heat to high. In a small bowl, combine cornstarch and water until smooth; stir into slow cooker. Cover and cook for 30 minutes or until thickened, stirring once. Serve over rice if desired. Sprinkle with raisins and coconut.

Prawns Curry

Ingredients

- 1/2 cup rice flour
- 1/2 teaspoon ground turmeric salt to taste
- 1 pound peeled and deveined prawns
- 3 tablespoons cooking oil
- 1 teaspoon cumin seeds
- 2 large onions, sliced thin
- 2 green chile peppers, halved lengthwise
- 1 tablespoon ginger-garlic paste
- 3 cups pureed tomato
- 1/2 teaspoon Kashmiri red chili powder
- 1/2 teaspoon garam masala
- 1/2 teaspoon ground cumin

- 1/4 cup heavy cream (optional)
- 1/4 cup chopped fresh cilantro

Directions

1. Stir the rice flour, turmeric, and salt together in a bowl; add the prawns and turn in the flour mixture to evenly coat.

2. Heat 3 tablespoons oil in a large skillet over medium heat; fry the cumin seeds in the hot oil until they splutter. Add the onions, green chile peppers, and ginger-garlic paste; cook until the onions are browned, about 5 minutes. Stir the pureed tomato, Kashmiri red chili powder, garam masala, and ground cumin into the mixture.

3. Season with salt and continue cooking until the gravy thickens and the oil is released, 10 to 15 minutes. Pour the cream into the skillet and stir; lie the prawns into the mixture and continue cooking until the prawns are cooked through, 3 to 5 minutes more. Garnish with the cilantro to serve.

Curry Chicken Salad

Ingredients

- 3 cooked skinless, boneless chicken breast halves, chopped
- 3 stalks celery, chopped
- 1/2 cup low-fat mayonnaise
- 2 teaspoons curry powder

Directions

1. In a medium bowl, stir together the chicken, celery, mayonnaise, and curry powder.

Mad's Peach-Curry Soup

Ingredients

- 5 tablespoons olive oil
- 2 tablespoons Madras curry powder
- 1 large onion, minced
- 3 cloves garlic, minced
- 1 (15 ounce) can sliced peaches in syrup, chopped
- 1 (14.5 ounce) can chopped plum tomatoes
- 1 teaspoon ground ginger
- 1 cup cream
- 1 cup vegetable broth
- salt and black pepper to taste
- 2 cups lettuce, chopped
- 2 cups shelled, cooked shrimp

Directions

2. Heat the oil in a large saucepan over medium heat; stir in the curry and cook 1 minute. Add the onion and garlic; cook 8 to 10 minutes, or until the onion becomes transparent. Stir in the peaches, including their syrup, with the tomatoes, ginger, cream, broth, salt, and pepper. Simmer over low heat for 45 minutes. Serve hot, topped with shrimp and lettuce.

Easy Chickpea Curry

Ingredients

- 1 tablespoon butter
- 1 onion, chopped
- 3 cloves garlic, minced
- 3 teaspoons curry powder
- 2 teaspoons garam masala
- 1/2 teaspoon ground paprika
- 1/2 teaspoon white sugar
- 1/2 teaspoon ground ginger
- 1/4 teaspoon ground turmeric
- 1/4 teaspoon salt
- 1/4 teaspoon pepper
- 1 (15 ounce) can garbanzo beans, drained
- 2 potatoes, chopped

- 1 (14 ounce) can coconut milk
- 1 tomato, chopped
- 1/3 cup milk
- 2 tablespoons ketchup
- 2 tablespoons sour cream
- 2 cubes chicken bouillon
- 1/4 cup ground almonds, or as needed

Directions

1. Melt the butter over medium heat in a large saucepan. Cook and stir the onion and garlic in the melted butter for about 5 minutes, until onion is translucent. Sprinkle in curry powder, garam masala, paprika, sugar, ginger, turmeric, salt, and pepper. Continue to cook and stir 3 to 4 more minutes, until spices are lightly toasted.

2. Mix in the garbanzo beans, potatoes, coconut milk, tomato, milk, ketchup, sour cream, and bouillon cubes. Simmer the curry over medium-low heat for about 25 minutes, until the potatoes are tender. Stir in ground almonds to thicken.

Vegetarian Bean Curry

Ingredients

- 2 tablespoons olive oil
- 1 large white onion, chopped
- 1/2 cup dry lentils
- 2 cloves garlic, minced
- 3 tablespoons curry powder
- 1 teaspoon ground cumin
- 1 pinch cayenne pepper
- 1 (28 ounce) can crushed tomatoes
- 1 (15 ounce) can garbanzo beans, drained and rinsed
- 1 (8 ounce) can kidney beans, drained and rinsed
- 1/2 cup raisins
- salt and pepper to taste

Directions

1. Heat the oil in a large pot over medium heat, and cook the onion until tender. Mix in the lentils and garlic, and season with curry powder, cumin, and cayenne pepper. Cook and stir 2 minutes. Stir in the tomatoes, garbanzo beans, kidney beans, and raisins. Season with salt and pepper. Reduce heat to low, and simmer at least 1 hour, stirring occasionally.

Vegetarian Chickpea Curry with Turnips

Ingredients

- 2 tablespoons olive oil
- 1/2 onion, diced
- 2 cloves garlic, minced
- 1 tablespoon ground cumin
- 2 tablespoons curry powder
- 1 (15 ounce) can garbanzo beans (chickpeas), undrained
- 1/2 red bell pepper, diced
- 1/2 turnip, peeled and diced
- 1 cup corn kernels
- 1/2 (15 ounce) can tomato sauce
- 1 pinch crushed red pepper flakes (optional)

- 1 pinch salt
- 1 pinch cracked black pepper

Directions

1. Heat the olive oil in a large saucepan over medium heat. Stir in the onion, garlic, cumin, and curry powder; cook and stir until the onion has softened and turned translucent, about 5 minutes. Add the garbanzo beans, red bell pepper, turnip, corn, and tomato sauce.
2. Season with red pepper flakes, salt, and black pepper. Bring to a simmer over medium-high heat, then reduce heat to medium-low, cover, and simmer until the vegetables are tender and the curry has thickened, 1 1/2 to 2 hours.

Spinach-And-Berries Salad With Non-Fat Curry

Ingredients

- 6 ounces fresh spinach, torn in bite-sized pieces
- 1 cup thickly sliced strawberries
- 1 cup blueberries

- 1 small red onion, thinly sliced, pulled into rings
- 1/2 cup chopped pecans
- Non-Fat Curry Dressing
- 2 tablespoons balsamic vinegar
- 2 tablespoons rice vinegar
- 4 teaspoons honey
- 1 teaspoon curry powder
- 2 teaspoons Dijon mustard
- Salt, pepper to taste

Directions

1. Wash and dry spinach. Whip together dressing. Add to spinach and toss lightly. Add berries, onion and pecans. Toss lightly.

Spicy Dry Fried Curry Chicken

Ingredients

- 1 (2 to 3 pound) whole chicken
- 1/2 teaspoon ground turmeric
- 1 tablespoon ground coriander
- 2 teaspoons black pepper

- 1 1/2 tablespoons chili powder
- 1 1/2 teaspoons salt
- 3 tablespoons vegetable oil
- 1 teaspoon mustard seeds
- 1 teaspoon fenugreek seeds
- 1 large onion, sliced
- 1 1/2 teaspoons cumin seeds
- 3 leaves fresh curry
- 2 teaspoons ginger paste
- 1 teaspoon garlic paste
- 2 cups water
- 1 cup coconut milk
- 2 tablespoons fresh lime juice

Directions

1. Clean, and cut chicken into 12 to 14 pieces. Place chicken in a large bowl, and season with turmeric powder, coriander powder, black pepper, chili powder, and salt. Cover bowl, and refrigerate for 1 hour.

2. Heat oil in a large pan over medium heat. Fry mustard seeds, fenugreek, onion, cumin seeds, and curry leaves inn oil for about 3 to 4 minutes. Stir in garlic and ginger pastes, and cook for another 2 minutes. Add chicken

and water, stir, and cover with lid. Cook for 20 to 25 minutes.

3. Stir in coconut milk, and cook until almost dry. Stir to keep the chicken from sticking to the bottom of the pan. Stir in lime juice, and cook until dry.

Rajma (Kidney Bean Curry)

Ingredients

- 2 cups dry red kidney beans
- 1 large onion, chopped
- 4 cloves garlic, chopped
- 1 (2 inch) piece fresh ginger root, chopped
- 2 tablespoons vegetable oil
- 2 teaspoons ghee (clarified butter)
- 2 dried red chile peppers, broken into pieces
- 1 teaspoon cumin seeds
- 6 whole cloves
- 1 teaspoon ground turmeric
- 1 teaspoon ground cumin

- 1 teaspoon ground coriander
- 2 tomatoes, chopped
- 2 cups water
- 1 teaspoon white sugar salt to taste
- 2 teaspoons garam masala
- 1 teaspoon ground red pepper
- 1/4 cup cilantro leaves, chopped

Directions

1. Place the kidney beans into a large container and cover with several inches of cool water; let stand 8 hours or overnight. Drain and rinse.
2. Grind the onion, ginger, and garlic into a paste using a mortar and pestle.
3. Heat the oil and ghee together in a pressure cooker over medium heat. Fry the red chile peppers, cumin seeds, and whole cloves in the hot oil until the cumin seeds begin to splutter; stir the onion paste into the mixture and cook, stirring frequently, until golden brown. Season with the ground turmeric, ground cumin, and ground coriander; continue cooking for a

few more seconds before adding the tomatoes. Cook until the tomatoes are completely tender.

4. Add the drained kidney beans to the pressure cooker with enough water to cover; pour the 2 cups water additionally to the cooker.

5. Add the sugar and salt. Close the pressure cooker and bring to 15 pounds of pressure; cook about 40 minutes. Lower the heat to low and cook another 10 to 15 minutes. Release the pressure and open the cooker. Stir the garam masala and ground red pepper into the bean mixture; garnish with chopped cilantro to serve.

Sweet Lamb Curry

Ingredients

- 3 tablespoons all-purpose flour
- salt and black pepper to taste
- 3 1/2 pounds cubed lamb stew meat
- 6 tablespoons butter, divided
- 2 large onion, chopped
- 2 tablespoons brown sugar

- 3 tablespoons curry powder
- 1 large Granny Smith apple - peeled, cored, and cubed
- 1 cup chicken stock
- 1/2 cup raisins
- 1 tablespoon lemon juice

Directions

1. Place the flour in a plastic bag; season to taste with salt and pepper. Add the lamb, and shake until evenly coated with flour. Melt half of the butter in a large pot over medium-high heat. Cook the lamb in batches until golden brown on all sides, about 5 minutes per batch; set aside.

2. Reduce heat to medium and add the remaining butter. Stir in the onions, and cook until the onions have softened and turned translucent, about 5 minutes. Stir in the brown sugar, curry powder, apples, chicken stock, raisins, and browned lamb. Bring to a boil over medium-high heat, then reduce heat to medium-low, cover, and simmer until the lamb is very tender, 1 to 1 1/2 hours. Stir in the lemon juice and cook 2 minutes before serving.

Spinach Salad with Curry Vinaigrette

Ingredients

- 1/4 pound slab bacon
- 1 tablespoon curry powder
- 3 tablespoons red wine vinegar
- 1 tablespoon prepared Dijon-style mustard
- 9 tablespoons vegetable oil
- salt and pepper to taste
- 12 cups flat leaf spinach - rinsed, dried and stems removed
- 12 fresh mushrooms, sliced

Directions

1. Trim the rind from the bacon and cut into 1 inch cubes. Place bacon in a large, deep skillet. Cook over medium high heat until brown and crispy. Cover and reduce heat to lowest setting to keep bacon warm.
2. In a small, dry skillet, toast curry powder over medium heat, stirring often, until fragrant, about 30 seconds. Remove from heat.
3. In a medium bowl, whisk together the vinegar and mustard. Add oil in a thin stream, whisking constantly, until the oil is completely incorporated. Add curry powder and whisk until smooth. Season to taste with salt and pepper.
4. In a large bowl, toss together the bacon, spinach, mushrooms and vinaigrette until evenly coated. Adjust salt and pepper to taste and serve immediately.

Curry Meat Loaf

Ingredients

- 2 eggs
- 1/2 cup soft bread crumbs
- 1 envelope Italian salad dressing mix
- 1 1/2 pounds lean ground beef

- 2 cups crushed seasoned stuffing
- 1/2 cup finely chopped celery
- 1/2 cup mayonnaise
- 1/2 cup boiling water
- 1 teaspoon curry powder
- 1/2 cup apricot preserves

Directions

1. In a bowl, combine the first three ingredients. Crumble beef over the mixture and mix well. On a large piece of heavy-duty foil, pat beef mixture into a 10-in. x 8-in. rectangle. Combine the stuffing mix, celery, mayonnaise, water and curry powder; spoon down center of rectangle. Bring long sides over stuffing mixture, peeling foil away while folding. Seal edge and ends. Place seam side down in a greased 13-in. x 9-in. x 2-in. baking pan.
2. Bake, uncovered, at 350 degrees F for 45 minutes. Meanwhile, in a small saucepan, heat preserves; stir to break up pieces of fruit.
3. Spread over the meat loaf. Bake 10-15 minutes longer or until meat is no longer pink and a meat thermometer reads 160 degrees F.

German Currywurst

Ingredients

- 3 (15 ounce) cans tomato sauce
- 1 pound kielbasa
- 2 tablespoons chili sauce
- 1/2 teaspoon onion salt
- 1 tablespoon white sugar
- 1 teaspoon ground black pepper
- 1 pinch paprika
- Curry powder to taste

Directions

1. Preheat oven to Broil/Grill.

2. Pour tomato sauce into a large saucepan, then stir in the chili sauce, onion salt, sugar and pepper. Let simmer over medium heat, occasionally stirring; bring to a gentle boil and reduce heat to low. Simmer another 5 minutes.

3. Meanwhile, broil/grill kielbasa sausage for 3 to 4 minutes each side, or until cooked through. Slice into pieces 1/4 inch to 1/2 inch thick.

4. Pour tomato sauce mixture over sausage, then sprinkle all with paprika and curry powder and serve.

Rob's Lamb Curry Pie

Ingredients

Filling:

- 3 tablespoons olive oil
- 3 cloves garlic
- 1 (3/4 inch thick) slice fresh ginger root, coarsely chopped
- 1 tablespoon red curry paste
- 1/2 cup fresh cilantro leaves
- 1/2 teaspoon ground cumin
- 1/2 teaspoon ground turmeric
- 1/2 teaspoon cayenne pepper

- 1/4 teaspoon ground cinnamon
- 3 red onions, chopped
- 1 eggplant, chopped
- 3/4 cup chopped celery
- 1 large red bell pepper, chopped
- 3 cups diced leftover roast lamb

Sauce:

- 1 1/2 cups milk
- 3 tablespoons butter
- 1/2 cup sweet white wine
- 3 tablespoons all-purpose flour
- salt to taste

Crust:

- 1 cup all-purpose flour
- 1/2 teaspoon salt
- 1 tablespoon curry powder
- 6 tablespoons shortening
- 3 tablespoons cold water, or as needed

Directions

1. Preheat an oven to 375 degrees F (190 degrees C). Grease a large pie plate or baking dish.

2. Place olive oil, garlic, ginger, curry paste, cilantro, cumin, turmeric, cayenne pepper, and cinnamon into the work bowl of a food processor, and process into a paste. Place the curry paste into a large mixing bowl, and stir with red onions, eggplant, celery, and red bell pepper to coat all the vegetables with curry mixture. Turn the vegetables into a large skillet over medium heat, and cook and stir until the vegetables are tender, about 7 minutes. Stir in the cooked lamb, and cook and stir until the lamb is hot and coated with spice mixture, 2 to 3 more minutes. Turn off the heat under the skillet.

3. Heat milk, butter, and wine in a saucepan over medium heat until the mixture is hot but not boiling, and the butter is melted. Whisk 3 tablespoons of flour into the hot milk mixture, and cook, whisking constantly, until the sauce has thickened. Turn the heat under the skillet of lamb and vegetables to medium, and cook and stir until hot, about 2 minutes; pour the sauce into the lamb and vegetables, and stir to combine. Season to taste with salt, and pour the hot filling into the prepared pie plate.

4. To make crust, mix together 1 cup flour, 1/2 teaspoon of salt, and curry powder in a bowl until thoroughly

combined. Cut in the shortening with a pastry cutter until the mixture resembles coarse crumbs. Sprinkle with water, and stir gently until the dough just comes together. Form into a rough ball, place on a floured work surface, and roll out into a crust to fit the pie dish. Lay the crust over the dish and lamb filling, crimp it to the dish with a fork, and cut several slits in the top of the crust.

5. Bake in the preheated oven until the crust is golden brown and the filling is hot, about 35 minutes. Let cool 7 to 10 minutes before serving.

Thai Shrimp Curry

Ingredients

- 1 tablespoon vegetable oil
- 1/2 pound large shrimp, peeled and deveined
- 2 cups frozen stir-fry vegetables, thawed
- 4 teaspoons cornstarch
- 1 1/2 cups COLLEGE INN® Culinary Broth, Thai Coconut Curry
- 1/4 teaspoon red pepper flakes

Optional Garnishes: Cilantro

- Fresh basil

Directions

1. Heat oil in large skillet. Add shrimp; stir-fry 2 minutes. Add vegetables; stir-fry 2 minutes.

2. Dissolve cornstarch in broth; add red pepper flakes. Add to skillet. Cook, stirring, until thickened. Serve over noodles or rice and garnish with fresh basil and cilantro, if desired.

Chicken Coconut Curry

Ingredients

- 6 bone-in chicken breast halves, skinless
- 3 medium carrots, chopped
- 3 stalks celery, chopped
- 2 medium onions, chopped
- 2 tablespoons ground curry powder
- 2 tablespoons all-purpose flour
- 1 tablespoon hot water
- 1 (10 ounce) can coconut milk
- 1/2 cup raisins

- 1/2 cup apples - peeled, cored and shredded

Directions

1. In a large skillet over medium heat, evenly brown the chicken breast halves. Mix in carrots, celery, and onions. Cook and stir until vegetables are tender.
2. In a small bowl, mix the curry powder and flour with hot water. Blend in coconut milk, forming a thick paste.
3. Mix curry powder paste, remaining coconut milk, raisins, and apple into the skillet. Thoroughly coat chicken with the mixture. Cover, and reduce heat. Simmer 30 to 45 minutes, until chicken is no longer pink and juices run clear.

Chicken Chutney Sandwiches with Curry

Ingredients

- 1 roasted chicken, bones and skin removed, meat shredded
- 3/4 cup cranberry and apple chutney
- 1/4 cup whipped cream cheese
- 2 teaspoons curry powder
- 6 croissants, split

Directions

1. Stir together the chicken, chutney, cream cheese, and curry powder. Spread onto the split croissants and serve.

Chickpea Curry

Ingredients

- 2 tablespoons vegetable oil
- 2 onions, minced
- 2 cloves garlic, minced
- 2 teaspoons fresh ginger root, finely chopped
- 6 whole cloves
- 2 (2 inch) sticks cinnamon, crushed
- 1 teaspoon ground cumin
- 1 teaspoon ground coriander salt
- 1 teaspoon cayenne pepper
- 1 teaspoon ground turmeric
- 2 (15 ounce) cans garbanzo beans
- 1 cup chopped fresh cilantro

Directions

1. Heat oil in a large frying pan over medium heat, and fry onions until tender.

2. Stir in garlic, ginger, cloves, cinnamon, cumin, coriander, salt, cayenne, and turmeric. Cook for 1 minute over medium heat, stirring constantly. Mix in garbanzo beans and their liquid. Continue to cook and stir until all ingredients are well blended and heated through.

3. Remove from heat. Stir in cilantro just before serving, reserving 1 tablespoon for garnish.

Butter Chickpea Curry

Ingredients

- 4 medium potatoes, cubed
- 2 tablespoons canola oil
- 1 medium yellow onion, diced
- 1 teaspoon minced garlic
- 2 teaspoons curry powder
- 2 teaspoons garam masala
- 1 teaspoon ground ginger 1 teaspoon cumin

- 1 teaspoon salt
- 1 (10.75 ounce) can condensed tomato soup
- 1/2 cup cream or milk
- 1 (12 ounce) can chickpeas, rinsed and drained

Directions

1. Place potatoes in a saucepan, cover with water, and bring to a boil over high heat; simmer until the potatoes are tender. Drain, and set aside.
2. Warm oil in a skillet over medium heat. Stir in onion and garlic, and cook until the onions are soft and translucent. Stir in curry powder, garam masala, ginger, cumin, and salt. Cook for 1 or 2 minutes, stirring. Pour in soup, cream, and chickpeas. Stir in potatoes.
3. Simmer 5 minutes.

Fragrant Chicken Curry

Ingredients

- 2 tablespoons curry powder
- 1 teaspoon ground ginger
- 1/2 teaspoon ground cinnamon
- 1/4 teaspoon ground cloves
- 1/4 teaspoon cayenne pepper
- 2 tablespoons vegetable oil
- 1 large onion, halved and thinly sliced
- 3 garlic cloves, minced
- 1 rotisserie chicken, skinned and boned, meat pulled into large chunks
- 1 (13.5 ounce) can light coconut milk
- 1 (14.5 ounce) can diced tomatoes
- 1 (14.5 ounce) can chicken broth To serve:

- Cooked basmati rice chopped fresh cilantro mango chutney

Directions

1. Mix spices in small bowl. Heat oil in a Dutch oven or small soup kettle over medium-high heat; add onion and saute until golden, 8 to 10 minutes.

2. Add garlic; saute until fragrant, about 30 seconds. Add spices; toast until fragrant, 30 seconds to 1 minute. Add chicken; stir until completely coated with spices. Add coconut milk, tomatoes and broth. Bring to a simmer; cook uncovered until flavors blend and stew is thick, about 20 minutes.

3. Remove from heat, sprinkle with cilantro and serve over rice. Pass chutney separately.

Delightful Indian Coconut Vegetarian Curry

Ingredients

- 5 russet potatoes, peeled and cut into 1-inch cubes
- 1/4 cup curry powder
- 2 tablespoons flour
- 1 tablespoon chili powder
- 1/2 teaspoon red pepper flakes
- 1/2 teaspoon cayenne pepper
- 1 large green bell pepper, cut into strips
- 1 large red bell pepper, cut into strips
- 1 (1 ounce) package dry onion soup mix (such as Lipton®)
- 1 (14 ounce) can coconut cream water, as needed
- 1 1/2 cups matchstick-cut carrots

- 1 cup green peas (optional)
- 1/4 cup chopped fresh cilantro

Directions

1. Place the potatoes into the bottom of a slow cooker.
2. Mix the curry powder, flour, chili powder, red pepper flakes, and cayenne pepper together in a small bowl; sprinkle over the potatoes. Stir the potatoes to coat evenly. Add the red bell pepper, green bell pepper, onion soup mix, and coconut milk; stir to combine.
3. Cover the slow cooker and cook on Low until the mixture is bubbling, adding water as needed to keep moist, 3 to 4 hours. Add the carrots to the mixture and cook another 30 minutes. Stir the peas into the mixture and cook until the vegetables are tender to your liking, about 30 minutes. Garnish individual portions with cilantro to serve.

Thai Red Chicken Curry

Ingredients

- 2 teaspoons olive oil
- 1 pound skinless, boneless chicken breast halves - cut into thin strips
- 1 tablespoon Thai red curry paste
- 1 cup sliced halved zucchini
- 1 red bell pepper, seeded and sliced into strips
- 1/2 cup sliced carrots
- 1 onion, quartered then halved
- 1 tablespoon cornstarch
- 1 (14 ounce) can light coconut milk
- 2 tablespoons chopped fresh cilantro

Directions

1. Heat the oil in a large skillet over medium-high heat. Add the chicken pieces; cook and stir for about 3 minutes. Mix in the curry paste, zucchini, bell pepper, carrot and onion. Cook and stir for a few minutes.
2. Dissolve the cornstarch in the coconut milk, then pour into the skillet. Bring to a boil, then simmer over medium heat for 1 minutes. Right before serving, stir in the cilantro.

Chicken Tikka Masala

INGREDIENTS

- 1 tbsp. extra-virgin olive oil
- 450 g boneless skinless chicken breasts, cut into 2.5cm cubes
- 1 onion, chopped
- 5 cloves garlic, crushed
- 1 tbsp. freshly crushed ginger
- 1/2 tsp. ground turmeric
- 2 tsp. ground cumin
- 2 tsp. paprika
- 2 tsp. garam masala
- 1 tsp. cayenne pepper
- 2 (400g) can chopped tomatoes

- 120 ml plus 2 tbsp. double cream
- Salt
- Freshly chopped coriander, for garnish
- Rice or naan, for serving

DIRECTIONS

1. In a large pan over medium heat, heat oil. Add chicken and cook, flipping once, until golden and no longer pink, 8 minutes per side. Transfer to a plate.
2. Add onion to pan and cook until soft, about 5 minutes. Add garlic, ginger, and spices and cook until fragrant, 1 minute. Add tomatoes and simmer until thickened, about 15 minutes.
3. Add double cream and chicken and simmer until warmed through, 5 minutes more. Season with salt.
4. Garnish with coriander and serve alongside rice or naan, if using.

Beef Massaman Curry

INGREDIENTS

- 90 g unsalted peanuts
- 1 (400ml) can coconut milk
- 800 g beef braising steak
- 20 ml vegetable oil
- 5 tbsp. curry paste (like Mae Ploy)
- 2 tbsp. fish sauce
- 2 tbsp. demerara sugar or palm sugar
- 400 ml water
- 1 tbsp. Tamarind paste
- 1 cinnamon stick
- 4 kaffir lime leaves
- 500 g waxy potatoes, cut into 3cm pieces

- 100 g green beans, cut into 2cm lengths
- 1 bunch coriander, finely chopped
- Jasmine rice, to serve
- Pak choi, to serve

DIRECTIONS

1. Heat a frying pan and toast the peanuts for 5 minutes, allow to cool and then roughly chop.
2. Open the can of coconut milk and scrape off the coconut cream. Add the cream into a heavy bottomed pan over a medium heat, (If using low fat coconut milk or it has not separated use 20ml vegetable oil).
3. Sear off the beef pieces in the pan until browned, then add the curry paste and cook for two minutes until the aromats are released.
4. Add the rest of the coconut milk, water, fish sauce, tamarind, sugar, cinnamon stick, kaffir lime leaves and half the peanuts and simmer for approx. 1.5 hours or until the beef is tender. Top up the pan a little with water if needed.
5. When the beef is ready add the potatoes cover and simmer for a further 15 minutes, then add the green beans and simmer for a further 5 minutes. Check the

potatoes and green beans are tender and season with further fish sauce if needed. Stir through the coriander.

6. Serve with Jasmine rice, pak choi and the remaining peanuts.

Chickpea Curry

INGREDIENTS

- 250 g brown rice
- 2 tbsp. extra-virgin olive oil
- 1 small red onion, halved and thinly sliced
- 2 small peppers (yellow, red, or orange), seeded and thinly sliced
- 3 cloves garlic, crushed
- piece fresh ginger, peeled and grated
- 1 tsp. curry powder
- 1 tsp. ground cumin
- 1/2 tsp. ground cinnamon
- 1/2 tsp. ground coriander
- 1/2 tsp. turmeric
- salt

- freshly ground black pepper
- 1 (400g) can chickpeas, drained and rinsed
- 1 (400g) can chopped tomatoes and juices
- 10 g freshly chopped coriander, plus more for serving

DIRECTIONS

1. In a medium saucepan, combine rice and 420ml water and bring to a boil. Reduce heat and simmer, covered, 30 minutes. Remove from heat and keep covered until ready to eat.

2. Meanwhile, make curry: In a large skillet over medium-high heat, heat oil. Add onion and peppers and cook, stirring occasionally, until soft, 7 to 8 minutes. Add garlic and ginger and cook until fragrant, 1 minute. Add curry powder, cumin, cinnamon, coriander, and turmeric and cook, stirring constantly, until fragrant, 2 minutes. Season with salt and pepper.

3. Stir in chickpeas and tomatoes and bring mixture to a boil. Reduce heat to low and simmer, uncovered, until thickened, 10 minutes. Stir in cilantro and season with salt and pepper.

4. Fluff rice with a fork and season with salt. Serve with curry and garnish with coriander.

Sag Aloo

INGREDIENTS

FOR THE CURRY BASE

- 700 ml water
- 25 g ginger, peeled and roughly chopped
- 2 onions, roughly chopped
- 1/2 tsp. cumin powder
- 1/2 tsp. coriander powder
- 1/2 tsp. turmeric
- 1/2 tsp. salt
- 50 ml vegetable oil
- 2 plum tomatoes, roughly chopped
- 800 g waxy potatoes, peeled and in 3 cm pieces
- 1/2 tsp. turmeric
- 7 tbsp. vegetable oil

- 1 green chilli, seeded and finely diced
- 1/2 onion, diced
- 3 cloves garlic, chopped
- 2 cm piece of ginger, peeled and finely diced
- 1/2 tsp. ground cumin
- 1/2 tsp. ground coriander
- 1/2 tsp. fenugreek seeds
- 1 tsp. mustard seeds
- 1 tsp. garam masala
- 1/2 tsp. chilli powder
- 1/2 tbsp. tomato puree mixed with 3 tbsp water
- 200 g kale, blanched
- 3 tsp. sea salt
- Handful chopped coriander

DIRECTIONS

TO MAKE THE CURRY BASE

1. Heat the water in a large saucepan. Add all the ingredients apart from the tomatoes and simmer covered for 45 minutes until the onions become very soft. Add the tomatoes and cook for a further 15 minutes.

2. Remove from heat and blend to a smooth consistency in a blender, or with a hand blender. This is now your simple curry base. You will have more than you need but it can be frozen for use in the future.

TO MAKE THE SAG ALOO

1. In a large pan of boiling water, add your potatoes, and turmeric. Simmer for approximately 20 minutes or until just tender but not falling apart. Drain and allow to cool.

2. In a heavy-based frying pan heat 4tbsp oil over medium heat. Add your cooked potatoes and fry until they have browned slightly but are not falling apart. Remove from pan.

3. In the same pan, add remaining 2tbsp oil, green chilli, onion, garlic and ginger. Cook gently until soft about 2-3 minutes.

4. Then, add all the spices and fry for about 30 seconds until the spices begin to darken. Add tomato puree and turn up the heat to slightly caramelise the onions.

5. Add 350ml of curry base, salt, potatoes, and blanched kale and cook on low for 5min, until potatoes are

heated through. Finish with handful of coriander. Serve.

Lightning Source UK Ltd.
Milton Keynes UK
UKHW021842070422
401245UK00008B/1778